Holy Moses

A Family-Focused Lenten Series

Arley K. Fadness

CSS Publishing Company, Inc., Lima, Ohio

HOLY MOSES

For more information about CSS Publishing Company resources, visit our website at www.csspub.com or email us at custserv@csspub.com or call (800) 241-4056.

Cover design by Barbara Spencer
ISBN-13: 979-0-7880-2432-9
ISBN-10: 0-7880-2432-9

PRINTED IN U.S.A.

Dedicated to my friends and colleagues
who are not afraid to step out of the box
and try ministries, programs, and processes
that promise to bring new life and joy
to individuals, families, and congregations.

Table Of Contents

Preface

Holy Moses is a joyful six session series that enlivens the spirit of children and adults alike as they relive and retell the greatest Salvation Event in the Old Testament — the Exodus of the Hebrew people from slavery. Through song, sermon, drama, and a "Moses" actor, the Exodus experience is remembered and applied to the lives of modern Christians.

Our test congregation at Good Shepherd Lutheran in Bismarck, North Dakota, a congregation of over 3,500 members, grew more excited each week drawing young and old along with many families. Two Lenten worships each midweek night became necessary to accommodate the worshipers.

Ed Johnson from Hill City and I (Arley Fadness) had a ball writing the words and music for *Holy Moses*. The theme song, "Holy Moses," when sung a time or two promises to stay with you as you hum it long after the worship is over.

Ed Johnson

Desert Rumblings (Holy Moses)

1.First no straw to make our earth - en brick, and then there's
2.Fire by night and it's that cloud by day, is that be -
piano

plagues and plagues, e - nough to make you sick. Frogs and gnats, there's flies and
cause your God thinks we can't find our way? Ev - ry day it's man - na,
piano

lo - custs too. Our life was real - ly bet - ter be - fore
what a thrill, I think we all would set - tle for some
piano

18
we met you!
good road kill!
18
piano
20
Coda
com - ing next!
20
Coda
piano

Schedule

Lent 1	A Prince Is Born In Egypt
Midweek Lent 2 Worship	The Call To Moses
Midweek Lent 3 Worship	Deliverance!
Midweek Lent 4 Worship	Wilderness Wanderings
Midweek Lent 5 Worship	The Ten Commandments
Midweek Lent 6 Worship	News From The *Desert Times*

Versicle
(Holy Moses)

text: Arley Fadness
music: Ed Johnson

Versicle
(Holy Moses)

text: Arley Fadness
music: Ed Johnson

Word of grace
Congregation:
as You in - struct us in this
Piano.
place.
Pastor:
Glor - y to You, Fath - er,
Piano.
Son and Ho - ly Spir - it
Congregation:
glor'-ous Trin - it - y, three in one. A - men.
Piano.

Holy Moses

text: Arley Fadness
music: Ed Johnson

Holy Moses

text: Arley Fadness
music: Ed Johnson

1.Mos - es pulled up from the Nile, Hid from - Phar - oh 'cause
2.God calls from a burn - ing bush, Mos - es needs an e -
3.Grum - ble, grum - ble what a pain in the de - sert what's
4.Thun - der, light - ning lots of noise leaves a per - son with -
5.Aar - on, Aar - on, make a god, gold or sil - ver,
Pno.
he's so vile Then five wom - en, brave and strong de -
nor - mous push. Oh, God, why me, and why now? Ex -
there to gain. Snakes and cac - tus. sand and grit. the
out much poise. On Si - nai's height, way out of sight the
clay or sod. A gold - en calf he did make but
Piano
fied those who would do Mos - es wrong.
cu - ses gone - God shows 'em how.
bronze snake heals when you've been bit.
Lord God gave ten com - mands so right.
un - like Yah - wah it was a fake.
Piano

23
Coda
prom - ised land.
23
Piano

Manna Minute Suggested Activities

Bitter Water Sweet

- Senior citizens hand out small bottles of water to children and perhaps everyone
- Quilters collect dimension-specific square pieces of colored cloths from children to be made into blankets that week and presented the following week

Homeless

- Make Habitat Houses to hand out to the children
- Quilters collect cloth

The Role Of The Lamb

- Teenagers hand out Heifer Project International rubber animals/pins
- Quilters collect cloth and display new blanket(s)

Manna From Heaven

- Elders collect canned food for the food pantry from children
- Quilters collect cloth and display new blanket(s)

Quails For Supper

- Quilters display blankets from children's cloth donations
- Set up food pantry display

Saved By An Image On A Pole

- Quilters display blankets from children's cloth donations

Sample Bulletin For Lent

Lenten Vespers
"Holy Moses!"

Prelude

Welcome

Versicle

Lenten Hymn

Confession And Absolution

Leader: Jesus, Lamb of God, bludgeoned and bloodied for our sins,

Congregation: We have something to say — we need to come clean.
Too long we have harbored resentments and anger against others,
Too long we have withheld hand and heart from the poor,
Too long we have suffered from greed, lust, and actions that shame.
Loving Lord, break open our secrets and cleanse us by the Holy Spirit.
Help us to sing and dance in the joy of unmitigated forgiveness.

Leader: God of grace and glory, we claim your promise of forgiveness and mercy — you truly make all things new.

Congregation: Thanks be to God.

Lesson(s)

Song Response

Prayer

Theme Song "Holy Moses"

The Story (Drama)

Sermon

Song

Manna Minutes (Intergenerational time with Moses)

Offering

Prayers

Blessing

Lenten Hymn

Postlude

A Prince Is Born In Egypt

Exodus 1—2:1-10

Characters

Narrator
King Pharaoh (also singing part)
Pharaoh's Daughter
Miriam
Shiphrah (nonspeaking)
Puah

Props

"The Nile" sign
Reeds

Setting

King Pharaoh's Egyptian court

Narrator: Good friends, I am your narrator for tonight's production titled, "A Prince Is Born In Egypt." The story begins in ancient Egypt. You find it recorded in the Holy Bible, the first and second chapters of the book of Exodus.

These are the names of the sons of Israel who came to Egypt with Jacob, each with his own household: Reuben, Simeon, Levi, and Judah, Issachar, Zebulun, and Benjamin, Dan and Naphtali, Gad and Asher. The total number of people born to Jacob was seventy. Joseph was already in Egypt. Then Joseph died, and all his brothers and that whole generation. But the Israelites were fruitful and prolific; they multiplied and grew exceedingly strong, so that the land was filled with them (Exodus 1:1-7).

Now a new king arose over Egypt who did not know Joseph. Neither did he appreciate the sons and daughters of their families who had now become the people of Israel. *(sniffs)* I smell trouble! *(melodrama music is played)* — a villain has arrived!

Scene 1

(King Pharaoh comes down the aisle with a flair, wearing a flowing cloak, evil painted eyes, and black moustache reminisent of the villain in a melodrama. He paces back and forth, with a worried look on face and a furrowed brow.)

King Pharaoh: Wouldn't *you* be worried? *(points to audience)* Wouldn't *you* wake up in a sweat in the middle of the night? Wouldn't you pray to every god you ever heard of? *(prays mockingly)* O Isis, O Zeus, O Astarte, O Baal — oh me, oh my. What am I gonna do? Look, the Hebrew people are exploding — more numerous and more powerful, perhaps, than us Egyptians. Look at 'em. *(points and scans over the audience)*

(Piano begins to play. King Pharaoh sings "Israel The Fruitful Nation.")

You know Reuben and Levi and Judah and Asher, and Zebulun, Simeon and Benjamin.
Now do you recall the most famous of all, the most famous nation of all?
Israel, the fruitful nation, grew and grew 'n' grew.
And if you ever saw them, you could hardly count that crew.
All of the sons of Jacob, sired children by the score,
So many Hebrew people, what's the use of anymore?
Then one dusty desert day, I, the Pharaoh came to say,
"Israel with your families, get to work! There's no more ease!"
Then how the nation jeered me, they disregarded my throne,
They groaned and groaned as I told them, "I will work you to the bone."

(Big finish — King Pharaoh freezes.)

Narrator: *(King Pharaoh pantomimes while Narrator speaks)* The king, upset and worried, devised a plan: Work them to death! Diminish them by making them slaves. By their sweat they would build the mighty supply cities — Pithom and Ramses for Pharaoh. O the king was ruthless ... *(King Pharaoh rubs hands together)* O the king was oppressive.... O the Pharaoh king made their lives bitter, bitter, bitter. *(King Pharaoh freezes)* But the harder they worked, the tougher they got. They multiplied! *(happy music)* They prospered! *(more happy music)* They grew stronger and stronger. So the king acted!

King Pharaoh: *(unfreezes)* Hey you two women ... *(Shiphrah and Puah appear)* Come over here. Who are you anyway and what are you up to?

Puah: *(bows)* Yes, your highness ... we are your humble citizens Shiphrah and Puah. We are midwives. We help with births ... we assist mothers ... as they deliver their babies ...

King Pharaoh: *(rudely)* Oh be quiet! Listen to me and listen good! *(all lean in to listen)* Because the Hebrews — those Israelites — are multiplying so rapidly and obviously thriving even more than us Egyptians, I want you to, to, to ah, ahem, kill every male you help deliver! Got it? *(points at them and freezes)*

Puah: Got it, your highness. *(bows and freezes)*

Narrator: But the midwives feared God more than Pharaoh and instead of killing the boys as soon as they were born, they let them live. And when the king found out — he was furious!

King Pharaoh: *(in a rage — all unfreeze)* Why have you done this? Why have you allowed the male boys to live? I thought I ordered you ...

Puah: *(bows and speaks from kneeling position)* Well, your honor, your highness, your excellency, your Pharaohship, ahem ... uh ...

(winks at audience and crosses fingers as she speaks) because the Hebrew women are so vigorous and not like the Egyptian women they deliver before we even get there ... so we're too late.

King Pharaoh: A likely story! We'll see! *(exits first, then women follow)*

Narrator: So God dealt well with the midwives; and the people multiplied and became very strong. And because the midwives feared God, God gave them families. Then Pharaoh commanded all his people, "Every boy that is born to the Hebrew you shall throw into the Nile, but every girl shall live" (Exodus 1:20-21).

(music)

Scene 2

("The Nile" sign crosses right to left.)

Miriam: *(enters)* Hello, my name is Miriam. *(waves)* I am the sister of a baby boy born in that troubled, terrible time in Egypt. Let me tell you what happened.

Narrator: "Now a man from the house of Levi went and married a Levite woman. The woman conceived and bore a son; and when she saw he was a fine baby, she hid him three months. When she could hide him no longer she got a papyrus basket for him and plastered it with bitumen and pitch; she put the child in it among the reeds on the river. His sister stood at a distance, to see what would happen to him" (Exodus 2:1-4).

(Miriam stands at the side of the stage behind reeds, obviously watching.)

Narrator: *(Pharaoh's Daughter pantomimes while Narrator speaks)* Pharaoh's daughter comes down to the Nile River *(show "The Nile" sign)* to bathe. *(Pharaoh's Daughter pretends to dry* *herself)* Pharaoh's daughter sees the basket. *(Pharaoh's Daughter pretends to see basket)* She sees the baby. *(Pharaoh's Daughter points)*

Pharaoh's Daughter: This must be one of the Hebrew children.

Miriam: Shall I go and find a nurse from the Hebrew women to nurse the child for you?

Pharaoh's Daughter: *(nods head)* Why, yes, young lady, go fetch a nurse to nurse this beautiful little baby. *(oogles and ahhs over the baby)*

Miriam: *(turns to audience)* So I found our mother and I brought her to Pharaoh's daughter *(laughs)* and *our mother* took care of the little child *(whispers)*, my brother. Pharaoh's daughter even paid her to nurse little Moses. Yes, *Moses*, that was his name because it means, "I drew him out of the water."

(All stand and sing the "Holy Moses" theme song.)

Lent 1 Sermon

Pulled From The Nile

By faith Moses was hidden by his parents for three months after his birth, because they saw that the child was beautiful and they were not afraid of the King's edict.
— Hebrews 11:23

When one miner from the Sago mine was rescued after an explosion in a mine shaft recently, you may have recalled the dramatic rescue of Jessica McClure many years before. If you remember, Jessica was an eighteen-month-old child in Midland, Texas. In the late '80s she fell into a 22-feet deep well and was trapped for over two days. The entire community rallied to save her and eventually a paramedic pulled Jessica to safety from a newly drilled shaft.

Later, when asked "Who saved you?" Jessica replied, "Winnie-the-Pooh." What happened was that, while she was trapped in the well, a small speaker had been dropped down to her, and her mother kept singing her two favorite songs: "Jesus Loves Me" and "Winnie-the-Pooh."

Let us pray. Lord Jesus, some of us know what it feels like to be trapped in a dark and lonely place. Our traps can be of our own making — trapped in a well of fear, or chronic anxiety. When we feel the rising waters of insecurity and worry, save us by your almighty hand. In your gracious name we pray. Amen.

The River Nile is the longest river in the world. It snakes 4,160 miles from Burundi, Africa, to the Mediterranean Sea. In this exotic, life-giving river, lives one of the most fearsome creatures in the world — the *crocodilus Nilocticus* — the Nile crocodile. Twelve species of this strong, ferocious creature watch from the shoals, ready to spring and devour an unsuspecting animal or human.

It's hardly a place to hide a child — a beautiful child. In fact, nowhere in Egypt was it safe for a Hebrew child to be born and live under the Pharaoh Ramses II (1290-1224 B.C.E.).

During that time, in the twelfth century B.C., human crocodiles were on the prowl on the Nile banks, in the streets, in the back alleys with instructions to kill every Hebrew male child they could find. Pharaoh, as you heard, was paranoid over the rapid growth of the Hebrew people.

In this setting, a Hebrew couple from the tribe of Levi married. A beautiful baby was born to father, Amram, and mother, Jochebed (Exodus 6:20).

This child would not be left to the human crocodiles. This child was placed in a basket made with reeds from the Nile. It was a safe place. Besides, his sister, Miriam, kept a watchful eye.

The anonymous writer to the Hebrews explained, "By faith Moses was hidden by his parents for three months after his birth, because they saw that the child was beautiful and they were not afraid of the king's edict."

God used five strong women in the saving of this child. The first were two brave midwives — Shiphrah and Puah — they defied Pharaoh's orders and allowed the children to live.

The midwives feared God more than Pharaoh and every child that was born was saved. The third was the mother, Jochebed. She was motivated by faith to put away her fears. Jochebed could think of nothing but protecting her child, God's gift to her. Jochebed boldly became a risk taker and went against Pharaoh's killing frenzy.

Then there was Pharaoh's unnamed daughter. Unlike her murderous father, she is overcome with compassion as she approaches the Nile River for a bath. She takes pity on the child and orders him to be pulled out of the water. She adopts the child as her own. And he becomes a prince in the palace.

The fifth woman is the child's sister, Miriam. She watches from the shadows, ensuring that her brother will be safe. She steps forward. Miriam offers her own mother, the child's own mother, as a nurse.

Five women of faith, compassion, imagination, and ingenuity save the child whose name in Hebrew means "I drew him out." He is "the one drawn out." He is Moses! The literal meaning of Moses is "saved" or "delivered by God."

Your name and my name is Moses, too. We have been drawn out of the dangers of sin, death, and the power of the devil. Our Savior is not Winnie-the-Pooh, but Jesus the Christ.

Since 9/11 we have been threatened and terrorized. Uncertainty rules. Where and to whom do you look for safety and security?

A young, black convict was heard pleading as he was being executed in the South many years ago. He wept, "Joe Louis, save me, save me, Joe Louis." Joe Louis, the then heavyweight boxing champion of the world, was his only model of strength and power and salvation.

I want to be saved and safe from whatever would threaten me or my family. I yearn for hope and purpose. My hope is not built on my stocks, my military, or on human structures and institutions. In the end, all of that returns to dust. It becomes only ashes. My hope and salvation is simply built on Christ and him crucified.

One Sunday morning, Rocky O'Daniel was crossing the bridge over the Bad River near Fort Pierre, South Dakota, when he saw a boy had fallen into a hole in the ice. Eleven-year-old Tony Nye flagged Rocky down and said his playmate was drowning. "Help!" he pleaded. Mr. O'Daniel raced to the river, broke through the ice, and discovered it was his own son, Alan.

A garden hose was thrown out and both father and son were rescued.

When we know we are "Moses," too — delivered by God — we move forward in this Lenten season with joy and anticipation. Amen.

Israel, The Fruitful Nation

Lyrics:Arley Fadness
Music:Ed Johnson

12
intensely
Is - rael the fruit - ful na - tion grew and grew 'n grew.
12
piano

16
And if you ev - er saw them you could hard - ly count that crew.
16
piano

20
All of the sons of Ja - cob sir - ed child - ren by the score,
20
piano

24
So man - y Heb - rew peo - ple what's the use of an - y more?
piano
28
Then one dust - y des - ert day I, - the Phar - oh, came to say "Is - rael, with your
33
fam - i - lies, get to work! There's no more ease!" Then how the na - tion

37
jeered me; they dis-re-gard-ed my throne, They groaned and groaned as I
piano
41
told them: "I will work you to the bone!"
rit.
a tempo

Bitter Water Sweet

Object: small twigs (one for each person coming up front) and water in a small bottle or small bowl

Good evening. I am Moses, son of Jochebed and Amram, a prince in Pharaoh's palace for a time. I am the leader God called to lead the oppressed people of Israel out of the Egypt. I'm so glad to be here with you tonight. At this time I would like to invite children, teenagers, a few parents, and grandparents to come forward.

(traveling music)

Thank you for joining me. I've a story to tell. It happened after we left Egypt and found ourselves wandering in the wilderness of Shur. Oh, it was hot and dry. We were all thirsty. Three days out from Egypt and no water. Ever been so thirsty you would almost die for a drink?

Well, we found a place called Marah, but the water was bitter. We couldn't drink it. So I prayed to God and the Lord showed me a piece of wood like this only larger. *(show a twig)* I threw the wood into the bitter water and the water suddenly became sweet — so sweet we could drink it! And we all had a wonderful thirst-quenching drink. *(lap up a drink from a container)* Oh, how wonderful!

Now listen to this: People in many countries today do not have sufficient, unpolluted water to drink. They are poor and very thirsty. They need wells and clean springs. Sometimes they have to carry the water for miles. One way you can help make "bitter water sweet" like God did through me is to help them in Africa, Brazil, Haiti, and other places through well-drilling programs of Lutheran World Relief, Church World Service, Catholic Relief Service, Mennonite Central Committee, and other agencies.

By throwing a piece of wood into this basket *(hand out twigs to everyone)* — along with a donation of money for wells, new wells will be dug and their bitter lives can be made sweet. *(pass a basket through the congregation)*

Thank you. You may be seated. *(a prayer may be added here)*

(traveling music)

The Call To Moses

Exodus 2:11—4:17

Characters

Narrator
Moses
Voices (offstage)
Voice Of God (offstage)

Props

"Midian" sign
Staff
Tall stool
Sandals
Cloak or box (for snake)
Fake snake
White powder or white glove
Bush
Bright light

Setting

In the desert

(Moses is sitting stage right in costume on a tall stool but in a frozen position.)

Narrator: One day, after Moses had grown up, he went out to his people and saw their forced labor. He saw an Egyptian beating a Hebrew, one of his kinsfolk. He looked this way and that, and seeing no one, he killed the Egyptian and hid his body in the sand. When he went out the next day, he saw two Hebrews fighting; and he said to the one who was in the wrong, "Why do you strike your fellow Hebrew?" He answered, "Who made you a ruler and judge over us? Do you mean to kill me as you killed the Egyptain?" Then Moses was afraid and thought, "Surely the thing is known." When Pharaoh heard of it he sought to kill Moses (Exodus 2:11-15).

(A "Midian" sign is seen.)

Narrator: But Moses fled from Pharoah. He settled in the land of Midian and sat down by a well. The priest of Midian had seven daughters. They came to draw water, and filled the troughs to water their father's flock. But some shepherds came and drove them away. Moses got up and came to their defense and watered their flock. When they returned to their father Reuel, he said, "How is it that you have come back so soon today?" They said, "An Egyptian helped us against the shepherds; he even drew water for us and watered the flock." He said to his daughters, "Where is he? Why did you leave the man? Invite him to break bread." Moses agreed to stay with the man, and he gave Moses his daughter Zipporah in marriage. She bore him a son, and he named him Gershom; for he said, "I have been an alien residing in a foreign land" (Exodus 2:15b-22).

Narrator: After a long time the king of Egypt died. The Israelites groaned under their slavery and cried out.

(Offstage, Voices make groaning sounds.)

Narrator: Out of slavery their cry for help rose up to God. God heard their groaning, and God rememered his covenants with Abraham, Isaac, and Jacob. God looked upon the Israelites, and God took notice of them.

Scene 1

Moses: *(begins speaking, slowly taking center stage as he talks)* I was keeping the flock of my father-in-law, Jethro, who was the priest here in Midian. My job was to herd the sheep and one day I had gone into the wilderness with the flock near Horeb — they called Horeb the Mountain of God ... and ... something most amazing happened you'd hardly believe.

(Room is darkened. From stage right or stage left, a bright light appears brighter and brighter. Use a dimmer switch for the variation.)

Moses: An angel, most likely from the Lord, appeared in this flame of fire and brightness right out of a bush! And listen to this — I tell you the truth *(holds up right hand as if making a vow)* the burning bush was not consumed! And I said to myself I must turn aside — I must look at this great sight and see why the bush is not burning up. Then I heard this voice — it seemed to call out from the burning, fiery, flaming bush itself.

Voice Of God: Moses! Hey, hey, Moses!

Moses: Wha ... what? Uh, uh, here I am holy voice, holy bush, holy smoke ... uh ... whoever you are!

Voice Of God: Come no closer! Remove your sandals ... do it ... do it now ... this is holy ground!

Moses: Gulp, really? Holy ground? *(quickly takes off sandals and dramatically throws them high in the air and off to the side)*

Voice Of God: I am the God of your ancestors, the God of Abraham, the God of Isaac, and the God of Jacob! The cry of the Israelites has now come to me; I have also seen how the Egyptians oppress them. So come, I will send you to Pharaoh to bring my people, the Israelites, out of Egypt into freedom — the promised land!

Moses: Hey, wait, just *uno momento*, God of my noble ancestors (bows) Abraham, Sarah, Issac, Rebekah and all the rest ... who am *I* that *I* should go to mighty Pharaoh, eminent ruler of all Egypt, and bring the Israelites out of Egyptland? *(backs away from the light as he speaks until he is nearly offstage)*

Voice Of God: Don't sweat it, Moses. I, the God of your ancestors, Abraham, Isaac, and Jacob will be with you!

Moses: Oh, man! Uh, Mr. Voice ... I mean, the God of my Ancestors ... this is way, way, way too much! No way. No! No, no! *(after a long pause, reconsiders)* If, if I went to them ... what would I say?

Voice Of God: You say, "I Am Who I Am" has sent you!

Moses: I am who I am? What kind of an answer is that?

Voice Of God: Trust me. Just say, "I am who I am" has sent you! That's it!

(The light may change color for interest if you can snag a colored gel lens for your spotlight and/or flash the name Y – H – W – H on a screen or white wall.)

Moses: Okay, okay I got the name — now what?

Voice Of God: Go and assemble the elders of Israel, and say to them, "the Lord, the God of your Ancestors, the God of Abraham, of Isaac, and of Jacob, has appeared to me, saying: I have given heed to you in Egypt. I declare that I will bring you up out of the misery of Egypt ... to a land flowing with milk and honey. They will listen to your voice ..." (Exodus 3:16-18).

Moses: All right, I am who I am, but ... but I've got problems.

Voice Of God: What are they, Moses? Spit 'em out!

Moses: *(meekly)* But suppose they do not believe me or listen to me and say the Lord did not appear to me?

Voice Of God: What is that in your hand?

Moses: A staff!

Voice Of God: Throw it, throw it!

(Moses throws staff behind altar or curtain, then picks up a snake.)

Moses: Yikes! *(throws snake behind altar or curtain)*

Voice Of God: Now pick it up ... go ahead pick — it — up!

(Moses picks up staff now turned back.)

Moses: Whoa, whoa!

Voice Of God: Now put your hand inside your cloak.

(Moses puts hand in and it comes out white — use a white glove or some change agent.)

Voice Of God: Now put your hand back inside your cloak.

(Moses puts hand in and it comes out flesh color — remove white glove or change agent.)

Voice Of God: Now you see I will be with you and we will do marvelous things.

Moses: But, but I *cannot* speak very well. I am not eloquent!

Voice Of God: Very well, I give you your brother, Aaron, as your speaker. Use him. Any more excuses, Moses?

Moses: I guess not. *(freezes)*

Narrator: Moses is fearful. Every excuse displays his fear but every excuse is met with an answer to God's plan of deliverance. The purposes of I am who I am would not be thwarted. God in the heavens had heard the cry of the oppressed Hebrews in Egyptland and freedom was coming!

("Holy Moses" theme song)

Midweek Lent 2 Sermon

Can You Hear Me Now?

Exodus 3:1—4:17

Moshe Rabinea, they called him. Moses our teacher. Moses great lawgiver. Moses liberator. Moses patriarch. Moses leader of God's people — the Israelites. But few people remember Moses, the excuse-maker!

A cell phone commercial asks, "Can you hear me now?" The assumption is that one can hear anyplace, anytime, in any situation on this near-miraculous technology — the latest cell phone device and service.

When the voice of God comes from a burning bush that is not consumed, "Can you hear me now?" Moses finds excuse after excuse for not hearing nor listening to God's call.

The Lord God says, "I have seen the suffering of Israel so come, Moses, I will send you to Pharaoh to bring my People, the Israelites out of Egypt."

Moses replies, "Who am I? Who am I that I should go to Pharaoh, and that I should bring the children of Israel out of Egypt? I am nobody."

Ever felt that way? A nobody? Unimportant? A wallflower? A zero?

Ever felt like a letter addressed to "Occupant"?

Moses could have nominated any number of capable Israelites who were capable of leading the Hebrews out of Egypt. There was Korah, young Joshua, and any one of the elders. Was Moses still smarting from the time a Hebrew yelled at him at his fortieth birthday, "Who made you a prince and a judge over us?"

We are unsure who Moses knew, but we do know Moses knew himself. "I am nobody, Jehovah."

In his book, *Instrument of Thy Peace*, Alan Paton tells of a rabbi, a cantor, and a humble, synagogue janitor who are preparing for the Day of Atonement. The rabbi beats his breast and says, "I am nothing, I am nothing!"

The cantor likewise beats his breast and says, "I am nothing, I am nothing."

The synagogue janitor walks up and beats his breast and says, "I am nothing, I am nothing." And the rabbi looks over with disgust and says to the cantor, "Look, who thinks he is nothing!"

A second excuse Moses mumbles when God calls him to deliver the Israelites is just as lame. "I am ignorant. What if the Hebrew Elders should ask me, 'What is your God's name?' I don't have the information. I don't know enough." That is the excuse I used once when asked to teach a class in New Testament Koine Greek in one of my parishes. Actually, I was too lazy to brush up on my Greek and go for it.

The third excuse Moses uses is, "I am not convincing." Chapter 4, verse 1, "But suppose they will not believe me or listen to my voice?" Rabbinic legend tells us that it ultimately took one full year for Moses to convince the Egyptians to release the Hebrews and then to convince the Hebrews that he was, in fact, their leader.

The fourth excuse Moses uses is simply, "I can't talk. O my Lord, I have never been eloquent ... I am slow of speech and slow of tongue (Exodus 4:10). I can't."

But the Lord says to Moses, "Who gives speech to mortals? .... now go. I will be with your mouth and teach you what you are to speak" (cf Exodus 4:11-12).

Moses has still one more excuse, the final, ultimate excuse: "Please I'd rather not. Oh, my Lord, please send someone else."

Jill Briscoe wrote a book with a telling title, *Here Am I — Send Aaron.* We say, "Here I am, but send my pastor. Here I am, but send my spouse. Here I am, but please, Lord, I'd rather not!" Sound familiar? The excuses of Moses? I am nothing, I am dumb, I am not convincing, I can't speak, or I'd rather not.

But the truth of the matter is you are somebody God calls. Shoeless and humble we stand before God and God asks, "Can you hear me now?"

First John 3 says, "If our hearts condemn us, God is greater than our hearts." When our self feels small or fractured or isolated, we listen and we listen deeply. When we feel fearful, inadequate, small, or ugly, Paul says in 1 Corinthians, "Consider your call."

The Greek *Kletos* and *Klesis* is not a call to a task or an office but to a joyful relationship with God. Out of that relationship with God in Christ we sense our call. Our call is related to how God created us with certain spiritual gifts, talents, interests, abilities, personality, and passions.

So, how do I feel about myself?

How do I see myself?

Do I celebrate who I am?

Is my inner self and my outer self in sync, in harmony? Am I at peace?

No more excuses. No more self-loathing, self-deprecations, no more "poor me."

"I am nothing, I am nothing."

I will not be ruled by fear.

I live by the gift of faith. I am filled with the Holy Spirit by God's grace. I have confidence and courage to face whatever God calls me to face.

Walter Kallenbach was a noted musician, a trumpet soloist with Paul Whiteman. At the pinnacle of his popularity and success, Walter was blinded in a hunting accident. Later, Walter said the worst of it was not the blindness, but the self-pity he developed. His fiancée "Dear Johned" him. He fell into gloom and depression. However, in the midst of his despair, God found him, took hold of his life, and converted him. Walter went back to school, wrote nine books, and lectured before millions. He was acknowledged as America's number one man with a handicap.

Walter resisted excuses and self-pity and God used him in a marvelous way.

Listen, God is calling.

"Can you hear me now?" Amen.

Midweek Lent 2 Manna Minute

Homeless

Object: Habit for Humanity mementoes (contact local or national office to get these)

Good evening. I am Moses — Holy Moses — at least that's what some folks call me. I want to invite the children, moms and dads, teenagers, and a few grandparents up here in front with me.

(traveling music)

In my story in Exodus, God called me to lead the people of Israel out of Egyptland. God called me in that weird burning bush which was not consumed. But I had all kinds of excuses. I wondered and worried if I could actually bring the people of Israel out of Egypt. Would tough old Pharaoh let them go? Would the Israelites leave their comfortable homes? Leave their neighborhoods? Would they be willing to become homeless out in the wilderness?

In this Lenten season, you will have an opportunity to see that the Israelites were able to leave their homes for simply a promise. The promise was freedom and a land flowing with milk and honey.

I know that you know there are many homeless people today in your community and country. Millard Fillmore had a dream and he dreamed that every person could and should have an affordable home. So Millard, a convert to Christ, started Habitat for Humanity. Volunteers build homes for and with the homeless, and now tens of thousands of poor folks throughout the world are getting new homes. As a reminder that you can volunteer to help work with Habitat, I'll give you this memento from Habitat for Humanity. *(pass out mementoes)*

Let us pray: Dear Lord, as the Israelites left their homes with only a promise in their pockets, so give us the faith to step up and step out to help. In Jesus' name. Amen.

(traveling music)

Midweek Lent 3 Drama

Deliverance!

Exodus 7-12

Characters

Paulo (the producer)
Duke (the director)
Moses
Aaron
Pharaoh
Narrator
Mother
Children
Padre

Props

Movie studio equipment
Two director's chairs
Staff
Snake
Crown
Chair
Oversized Bible

Setting

Movie studio

Scene 1

Paulo: Hi, good morning, Duke.

Duke: Hi, yourself. Top of the morning, Paulo. Are you ready to go to work?

Paulo: Yep, and I'm excited. Making this epic movie about the great Hebrew exodus has me pumped.

Duke: Me, too. We make a good team. You, as the producer, and me as the director. Let's take our places. *(both sit in their respective chairs with backs to the audience)* The rehearsals were improving, a little shaky a time or two — now just a bit of fine tuning.

Duke: Camera, action, take one! *(snap, click)*

Scene 2

(Moses, Aaron, and Pharaoh appear in costume.)

Pharaoh: Okay you two — if you are really from the Hebrew God as you say you are — tell me *(sarcastically)* what's the god's name?

Moses: I am who I am.

Pharaoh: Whaaaa ... that's a name? Are you some Hebrew phonies? Let's see you prove this God even exists! Do a miracle, do some magic, so something — you fakers!

Moses: All right, your highness. Do it, Aaron.

(Aaron throws down his staff and it turns into a snake.)

Pharaoh: Ho, ho, my magicians, wise men, and sorcerers can do the very same thing. Call my magicians! Put out a call for my sorcerers! *(shouts)* Do the snake trick! We'll show you, Aaron and Moses, a thing or two.

(Actors freeze.)

Duke: Cut, cut! Great job! Moses speak up a little in the final take. Aaron straighten your robe and your beard. Camera crew ... get a good shot of the snake. But be careful!

Scene 3

Duke: This is scene three — take one. *(announces)* Moses and the plagues of terror. Action!

Paulo: Action!

Narrator: The first plague of the ten plagues was dramatic! Amazing! The Lord God of Israel instructed Moses to take Aaron's staff — the same staff that had turned into a slimy serpent and strike the Nile River! *(very dramatic)* When the sound of that staff hit the water, the water turned to ugly blood — red corpuscle blood — and the river began to stink because the red blood killed all the fish — they couldn't drink the water! Moses and Aaron did just as the Lord commanded in the sight of Pharaoh and all his Egyptian officials.

Moses: *(reprise)* Let my people go!

Pharaoh: *(haughtily)* No, no, no! No one leaves Egypt and surely not you — you Hebrew scum slaves! Get back to work! *(sings to the tune of* Showboat*'s "Old Man River")*

Tote that barge, lift those bales, get a little drunk and you land in jail.
Bake those bricks. Find your straw. Meet that quota, yeah, and you'll stay right here!

(speaks) Your lament — "We want to go out into the wilderness to sacrifice to our God" is just a lame, lazy excuse. Get to work!

(Actors freeze.)

Narrator: The second great plague was an invasion of ugly frogs. Yes, frogs. Frogs here, frogs there, frogs everywhere. On the floor, in their beds, in their ovens, in their soup. And when Pharaoh had had enough Aaron, spoke.

Aaron: All right, your highness, will you let our people go?

Pharaoh: Yes, yes. Get rid of this horrible invasion. I hate frogs. I hate frogs in my bed and in my closet, in my land. Go worship your God out in the desert. Get! Get!

Pharaoh: On second thought *(turns his crown around)* No! You can't go! Stay! Work!

Duke: Cut!

Paulo: Cut, cut! *(shoos actors and Narrator offstage)*

Duke: Now the story line continues in a modern setting. A faithful mother is reading this exodus story to her children. Action!

Paulo: Action!

(In comic relief, Duke looks over at Paulo mildly irritated.)

Scene 4

(Mother, holding an oversized Bible, is sitting in a chair with her children on the floor around her.)

Mother: *(reads to her children)* Then the Lord said to Moses, "Say to Aaron, 'Stretch out your staff and strike the dust of the earth, so that it may become gnats throughout the whole land of Egypt' " (Exodus 8:16) ... and all the dust of the earth turned into gnats, gnats, gnats ...

Child: Gnats, gnats, what are gnats, Mother? Are they like bugs or somethin'?

Mother: Gnats are insects — they bite, they irritate, they hurt both animals and humans and children — they were everywhere! So what did Pharaoh do?

Child: He let them go?

Mother: Yes, then he just played a mean, old game and jerked back his almost promise and said, "Nah, the Israelites could not go."

Child: What happened next?

Mother: Three more plagues — flies, disease, and boils. It was like a tug-of-war game. Pharaoh against Moses and Aaron.

*(**Option:** Moses and Aaron in aisle or background pulling on a rope in a tug-of-war with Pharaoh.)*

Duke: Cut right there!

Paulo: Cut right there!

Duke: *(comic relief)* Must you, Paulo, always repeat everything I say when I'm directing these scenes? The director, that's me, directs and the producer, that's you, produces.

Paulo: Got it, sir. I'll do better.

Duke: You'd better.

Paulo: Better.

Duke: Better. *(both laugh at each other)* On to scene 5. It's at church and the padre is giving a homily. Cameraman pans over to that scene.

(Padre enters.)

Scene 5

Padre: *(at a pulpit)* Now there was a seventh plague. It was thunder and hail. The Lord sent thunder and hail and fire on the land, such heavy hail as had never fallen upon the land of Egypt before. And mighty, old, stubborn Pharaoh said ... now I want you in the congregation to help me preach ... say, "No, no, no way Jose." *(directs the congregational response)*

Congregation: No, no, no way, Jose!

Padre: Very good. And when the Lord let the eighth plague locusts cover the land, old Pharaoh said ... *(directs congregation)*

Congregation: No, no, no way, Jose!

Padre: And when the Lord plunged all Egypt into darkness, the ninth plague, what did old Pharaoh say, but ... *(directs congregation)*

Congregation: No, no, no way, Jose!

Padre: Oh, the people yearned to be free. They wanted to be free, free at last. *(Martin Luther King Jr. style)* And finally, finally it came. *(sings "When Moses was in Egyptland ... let my people go ..." and walks out)*

Scene 6

Narrator: The final plague that would accomplish freedom for the Hebrew nation was a costly, deadly plague — the plague of death. Death to the firstborn in all the land. After Moses described the details of the coming of the angel of death and the way to escape by painting lamb's blood on the doorpost, he detailed the wonderful Passover.

Moses: You shall keep the lamb until the fourteenth day of this month, then the whole assembled congregation of Israel shall slaughter it at twilight. They shall take some of the blood and put it on the door posts and the lintel of the houses in which they eat it ... It is the passover of the Lord. "For I the Lord will pass through the land of Egypt that night and I will strike down every firstborn in the land of Egypt, but when I see the blood I will pass over you and no plague shall destroy you ..." (cf Exodus 12:6-12).

Narrator: And after the angel of death came, Pharaoh had had enough. *(buoyantly)* And the people of Israel packed up their belongings and left ... they were free!

(Duke and Paulo stand and applaud. They invite the congregation to stand and applaud.)

Duke: Now this will make a great movie, won't it?

(Sing the "Holy Moses" theme song.)

Midweek Lent 3 Sermon

Free At Last!

Exodus 12:13; Galatians 5:1; Luke 4:18, 19

Recently, a young man got stuck spelunking in the caves of the Black Hills. He was one of four teenagers from Rapid City who went caving for recreational adventure. Worming their way through dark passageways and tiny shafts like veteran speleologists (one who explores and studies caves) they wiggled and crawled until one of the four could go no further.

Three got out, but a rescue team had to go in under the direction of veteran spelunker, Steve Baldwin, and rescue him. The young teenager was unhurt, safe, and glad to be free.

It's a good thing he didn't suffer from claustrophobia. Claustrophobia is the fear of closed spaces, and if you have it spelunking is not your sport.

The people of Israel suffered from a crushing social claustrophobia — hemmed in and suffocated by the slavish demands of their Egyptian oppressors. They were in need of rescue. They wanted their freedom and they wanted it now!

Moses arrived on the scene and confronted mighty Pharaoh. But like two billy goats butting heads, stubborn Pharaoh slams Moses who defiantly insists, "Let My People Go!"

This tug-of-war between Pharaoh and Moses struggled through ten terrible plagues. First a staff slap on the River Nile turns the water blood red. "Thus says, the Lord God, 'Let my people go.' " But, Pharaoh's heart is hardened, "No way."

Then the second plague. Frogs were everywhere. Pharaoh said, "Okay go," but then changed his mind. "No way. Stay here." The tug-of-war continues. It's gnats and then flies, sick livestock, boils, incessant thunder and hail, locusts, and darkness. The tug-of-war goes back and forth. "Yes, go. No, you can't. Yes, go. No, you can't." Finally the time is up.

The final plague. The death of the firstborn — the final and most devastating of all, but God provides a way of escape for the people of Israel. It's blood. "Paint the blood of a lamb on your doorpost and the angel of death will pass over. The firstborn will be saved in your household." Night comes. A terrible wail is heard throughout Egypt. The firstborn are killed; even the cattle. But every household who observes the instructions and paints blood on the doorpost is saved. The angel of death passes over.

Pharaoh at last, had had it! "Go," he said to Moses and the Israelites, "Go — get out of here, worship the Lord as you said. Take your flocks and your herds as you said and be gone."

The Israelites were free. Free at last!

Now we jump centuries ahead to the New Testament. And we hear Jesus say in Luke 4, "The Spirit of the Lord is upon me, because he has anointed me to bring good news to the poor. He has sent me to proclaim release to the captives and recovery of sight to the blind, to let the oppressed go free...."

It is by the blood we are rescued, released, saved, and set free! The blood is on the doorpost and for us the blood is on the cross. The blood covers every sin in your life and mine.

Some time ago, two surgeons and an anesthetist took turns lying on the operating table beside a critically ill patient. They saved her life with direct transfusions of their own blood. The patient's blood had ceased to coagulate and only live blood would save her life. Their blood was life to her.

Christ's blood is life to you. It brings freedom from sin, death, and the power of the devil. No longer do you and I need to stay in the cave of sin and death. We feel claustrophobic in there. We are hyperventilating, but once rescued, we have air, space, and room to move. We need the sunshine. You and I are made for freedom.

But freedom for what? How free is freedom? Is it "anything goes?" Is it freedom to do as I please?" Or are there boundaries, limits, and fences in freedom?

Bob Bartlett, the explorer, told a story about a voyage one summer. He and his party brought back a large number of caged birds. Somewhere in the middle of the ocean, one restless bird escaped from his cage. In its newfound freedom, the bird flew happily away.

When he disappeared out of sight, the crew said, "That bird is lost." But after some hours had passed, to their surprise, they saw the bird again, coming toward the ship, exhausted. Panting and breathless, the little feathered prodigal dropped upon the deck. Far over the trackless, endless water, the bird had eagerly sought the ship again. The ship was no longer a prison. It was home — the only way across the deep.[1]

When Jesus preached his first sermon, he said he came to set the captives free. Yet, the first step he made in the process was to bind them to himself. To make himself their home. Their only way across the deep. "Follow me," he says. Follow me. There is no freedom except in the will of God.

That is the great paradox of freedom.

Freedom in Christ means we are free from the new demands and laws placed upon us. We are never free until we are bound, mastered by something greater than ourselves.

"Make me a captive, Lord, and then I shall be free."

"You are called to freedom," said Peter, "only use not your freedom for the flesh ... but love and be servants of one another."

In Christ we are free to love.

In Christ we are free to forgive.

In Christ we are free to share.

---

1. J. Wallace Hamilton, *Horns and Halos in Human Nature* (Westwood, New Jersey: Fleming H. Revell Company, 1954).

Midweek Lent 3 Manna Minute

The Role Of The Lamb

Object: Heifer Project International gift arks or small toy animals for each participant

Good evening. Holy Moses here again. Welcome to this wonderful Lenten worship. I am pleased to invite children, moms and dads, teenagers, and grandparents to come forward for a Manna Minute.

(traveling music)

You folks are getting ready for Holy Week during these forty days of Lent and that's wonderful! We just heard the story of how lambs were used to save the firstborn from the angel of death. It took the blood of a lamb painted on the door post to give safety. It was a terrible plague, but it finally jarred Pharaoh loose and he let the people go.

I am humbled to realize that I have been a part of God's greatest salvation event in the Old Testament. And in the New Testament Jesus becomes the Lamb of God which takes away the sins of the entire world.

Do you know that animals, though in a different way than the lambs in the Passover story, are saving human lives? Let me tell you about Heifer Project International. Through this Christian organization, one can give an animal to a poor family in a third world country and help them improve their livelihood.

I am handing out gift arks from HPI (or a small toy animal) to teach you about how you can support poor people. You can give a lamb, goat, a heifer, or a rabbit and help lift a poor family out of poverty and give them a new start. *(hands out objects)*

Thank you for coming forward tonight and considering the importance of lambs and the true Lamb.

(traveling music)

Wilderness Wanderings

(Photos In The Desert)

Exodus 15-16; Numbers 21:9

Characters

Photographer
Moses
Aaron
Hebrew 1
Hebrew 2

Props

3' x 6' cardboard or wood backdrop picture frame
"Elim" sign
Palm tree
Quail picture
Manna picture
Bronze serpent picture or representation
Camera (preferably an old time camera on a tripod with a hood)
Tree branch
Goblet

Setting

Wilderness

Scene 1

(Photographer enters and freezes; Aaron enters left, and Moses enters right.)

Moses: I am Moses. People call me Holy Moses. But let me tell you, I didn't feel so "holy" out there in the hot desert. Let me tell you the story and you'll know what I mean. We left Egypt dancing!

We Hebrews were free. Free at last. All the Israelites sang a song of deliverance thanking God. And my sister, Miriam, broke out into song, too. With tambourines and dancing, she sang, "Sing to the Lord, for he has triumphed gloriously; horse and rider he has thrown into the sea" (Exodus 15:21). Then three days in the wilderness a crisis hit! We were completely out of water.

All: Moan!

Moses: We came to a place called Marah, which means bitter. The pool of water there was horrible. We couldn't drink it. Oh, were we thirsty.

All: Moan!

Moses: And when the people complained, I threw this piece of wood *(hold up tree branch)* into the pool of water and the water amazingly turned sweet and drinkable. I had some myself. *(drinks out of a goblet)*

Photographer: *(unfreezes)* Hold it there. **Photo Shoot 1 — Moses holding a piece of wood and drinking from goblet.** *(flash)* Thank you, Moses, sir. The proofs will be in on Tuesday.

Moses: *(moves to stage left near "Elim" sign and palm tree)* Then we, and the whole Hebrew nation, went on in the wilderness and camped at a place called Elim. Beautiful place. Twelve springs of water and seventy palm trees. We had wonderful shade, a resting place, and blessed drink. God provided it. And God provided more than that. Listen to the problem that developed.

(Two angry-looking Hebrews appear.)

Hebrew 1: *(grumbling)* I've about had it. First no water, then this blazing sun — now we have come out to this desert place and nothing to eat!

Hebrew 2: *(whines)* If only we had died by the hand of the Lord in the land of Egypt, when we sat by the fleshpots and ate our fill of bread; for Moses has brought us out into this wilderness to kill this whole assembly with hunger (Exodus 16:3).

Hebrew 1: And we aren't the only ones complaining. Everybody is upset. They're hungry, too. What good is freedom when you're starving?

("Complaint Song" may be sung by the two angry Hebrews or a chorus of voices offstage.)

Chorus: Oh, woe is me, woe is us,
    Why can't we get on a bus (out of here)?

Verse 1: Please out of here, out of there,
    Seems like sand is everywhere.
    Grab a drink, not a drop
    We could use a soda pop! (Chorus)

Verse 2: My stomach growls, I feel faint.
    When I complain — I am no saint.
    Can't eat freedom, once so fine,
    back to Egypt where life's divine. (Chorus)

Photographer: Hold it right there. **Photo Shoot 2 — Hungry, complaining people.** *(flash)* Thanks, complaining Hebrews!

Moses: Then God, in God's amazing generosity and sensitivity, spoke to me, and I spoke in turn to my brother, Aaron. *(points to Aaron who stands stage right)*

Aaron: Tell the people God will provide. I have heard the complaining of the Israelites; say to them, "At twilight you shall eat meat, and in the morning you shall have your fill of bread; then you shall know that I am the Lord your God" (Exodus 16:12).

Moses: In the evening, quails *(holds up picture of quail)* that migrate across the Red Sea to Europe in the spring, land for the night. There is your meat. And in the morning when the layer of dew has lifted, you will find fine flaky parcels. It is bread, manna *(holds up picture of manna)*, and it is from the Lord. Eat your fill, you hungry Israelites! See God provides! Trust God. *(moves to stage right)*

Scene 2

Aaron: I'm Aaron, Moses and Miriam's brother. As you may know I was sort of the "mouthpiece" for my brother, Moses. Moses saw himself as slow of speech, at least at first. Some think that was just an excuse. Others believed him. I was glad to help out. *(poses for photographer)*

Photographer: Hold it right there. **Photo Shoot 3 — Aaron's portrait.** *(flash)*

Aaron: Now let me tell you of a hair-raising incident in the wilderness. It about scared the bejeebers out of Moses! Historians call it the bronze serpent incident. *(reads)* From Mount Hor we set out by the way to the Red Sea, to go around the land of Edom; but the people became impatient on the way. The people spoke against God and against Moses, "Why have you brought us up out of Egypt to die in the wilderness? For there is no food and no water, and we detest this miserable food" (cf Numbers 21:4-5).

Then the snakes came. Yikes! *(leaps around as if they are on stage)* Snakes everywhere — and they were poisonous. Bit Joseph and Levi and Joahi and ... oh it was terrible. *(reads)* Then the people came to Moses and said, "We have sinned against the Lord and against you; pray to the Lord to take away the snakes from us." So Moses prayed for the people. And the Lord said to Moses, "Make a poisonous serpent and set it on a pole and everyone who is bitten shall look at it and live." So Moses made a serpent of bronze, and put it on a pole; and whenever a serpent bit someone, that person would look at the serpent of bronze and live (cf Numbers 21:7-9).

Photographer: Picture, please. *(gives positioning instructions)* **Hold it! Photo Shoot 4 — Bronze serpent incident.** *(flash)* Thank you — I'll have a portrait in color of the bronze serpent for your future reference.

Scene 3

(Moses and Aaron together)

Moses: It was truly amazing. God, the one who said, "I am who I am," literally guided us every step on the journey in the wilderness.

Aaron: It was bleak at times. But our goal was the promised land. It took us, would you believe, forty years to get to the promised land.

Moses: And the distance was not that far, but the distance was in our hearts and God had to work on us in the wilderness.

Aaron: So we built a traveling tabernacle, a tent for meetings in which God met my brother, Moses, and Moses here *(points to Moses)*, answered the questions and solved the problems the Israelites brought to him.

Moses: Remember how the tabernacle was constructed, Aaron? You became a priest, you know, so you would remember, right?

Aaron: Yes, I do remember. The tabernacle was made of acacia wood, hair and skins of the flock, skins of animals, gold, silver, brass, and linen. It was simple, but beautiful.

Moses: And the purpose of it?

Aaron: You know, Moses. It housed the sacred vessels, showbread, and candelabrum.

Moses: Your role, Aaron?

Aaron: I, a descendant of the tribe of Levi, was entrusted with the ministry of the priesthood. I was appointed to care for the tabernacle along with my four sons, Nadab, Abihu, Eleazar, and Ithamar. I served as high priest for nearly forty years.

Moses: And over the tabernacle, God lead the entire people of Israel in an amazing way. God lead us by a cloud during the day and at night a column of fire.

Aaron: Yep. We camped.

Moses: We traveled.

Aaron: We stopped.

Moses: We complained.

Aaron: God dealt with us.

Moses: We moved on.

Moses and Aaron: God our leader and guide.

Photographer: Hold it, please. **Photo Shoot 5— Moses and Aaron, arm-in-arm, smiling broadly.** *(flash)*

(Sing the "Holy Moses" theme song.)

Midweek Lent 4 Sermon

Deliverance Again!

And just as Moses lifted up the serpent in the wilderness, so must the Son of Man be lifted up that whoever believes in Him may have eternal life.

— John 3:14, 15

Bob Hope made it to 100 years of age. Bob Hope, the king of laughter, movie star, singer, and dancer for all those 100 years surely must have gotten tired.

One night, Bob Hope reported his activity for the day. "Today," he said, "my heart beat 103,369 times. My blood traveled 168 miles. I breathed 23,040 times. I inhaled 438 cubic feet of air. I ate 3 1/4 pounds of food, drank 2 pounds of liquid. I perspired 1 1/2 pints. I gave off 85 degrees of heat. I generated 450 tons of energy. I spoke 4,800 words, moved 750 major muscles, and I exercised 7 million brain cells. My, I'm tired."[1]

The children of Israel were tired. Tired and crabby. Moses had led them out of slavery; set their feet on the road to freedom. It was a great moment in their history. But tired and discouraged, they began to behave badly.

Exodus 15 reveals how the long years of slavery had corroded them and bleached all the fight out of them. Now bitter water, no food, endless heat — you and I would get disheartened, too.

The people murmured against Moses. Captain Moses sensed mutiny — the crew felt the freedom ship was going nowhere. "... for you have brought us out into this wilderness to kill this whole assembly with hunger."

"It's easier," said the author, Stainer, "to get people out of slavery than to get slavery out of people."

The roads to nowhere are hard to make.

George Moore wrote a novel in which he tells of Irish peasants put to work building roads by the government during the Great Depression. At first, the crew worked well. Sang their Irish songs. Glad to be back at work again.

But, little by little they discovered that the roads they were building led nowhere, ran out in the bogs and stopped. As the truth gradually dawned on them that they had been put to work to provide them busy work and as an excuse to feed them, the men grew listless and stopped singing.

Commenting on the incident, George Moore said, "The roads to nowhere are difficult to make. For a person to work well and sing, there must be an end in view."

One day, the children of Israel came to Elim — an oasis in the desert. At Elim there were twelve springs of water and seventy palm trees — oh, blessed rest, relaxation, and refreshment. Their tiredness was gone, their bitter water made sweet, and shade from the scorching heat.

Israel began to sing again but not for long. It didn't last. Soon the Israelites were complaining, and the complaints against Moses were perceived as complaints against God.

Then from out of the rocks came the snakes. Poisonous snakes (Numbers 21:6), and they bit the people and many died. The people came to Moses and repented, "We have sinned against the Lord and against you."

So Moses prayed for the people and, instructed by the Lord, erected a great bronze serpent so that whoever had been bit and looked at it were healed and saved.

On one cover of a South Dakota magazine was a painted prairie rattlesnake. Articles depicted the rattler as a friend and as a foe. One story, by 103-year-old Emma Tomsik Streenz of Aberdeen, told of being bitten as a child on the western South Dakota plains by a rattler. She nearly died, but survived.

Some of the readers of the magazine were so incensed that the editor was brazen enough to picture a rattlesnake on the cover of his magazine they tore the cover off and sent it back with letters chastising him.

Most of us have strong feelings about snakes, especially poisonous ones that can do us harm. The appearance of the serpents in the Israelite camp was a judgment for their complaining and grumbling against Moses and against God.

Later, John wrote in his gospel that just as the bronze serpent was lifted up for the people to see, so was Christ lifted up on the cross to save all who believe.

In Christ we are refreshed, relaxed, and restored. Julia Ward Howe once slumped down in her chair and said, "I'm tired. I'm tired all the way down into the future ..." but she didn't stay there. She was a believer; she felt God's presence in her life. By faith in the divine purpose, she wrote the song that has since set folks marching and their blood tingling: "The Battle Hymn Of The Republic."

"Mine eyes have seen the glory of the coming of the Lord."

Isaiah was talking about the long march of the exiles when he wrote, "They will renew their strength, will mount up with eagles. They will run and not get tired."

The serpents of pessimism, discouragement, tiredness, and purposelessness threatened from every rock and hole.

When a volcano exploded on the Island of Martinque in the West Indies some years ago, the ecological balance went crazy. All jungle life sought refuge in the town of St. Pierre. First came the centipedes, ants, and insects. The people killed them with hot oil, fire, and boiling water.

Then a far greater danger appeared. The *fer-de-lances* came. These six-foot long, poisonous snakes killed horses, pigs, chickens, and more than thirty people. The soldiers tried to shoot them. But then an amazing thing happened. The cats of St. Pierre who roamed freely, were attracted by the noise. They teased and then killed the snakes by pinning their heads to the ground and breaking their vertebrae. Within an hour, 100 snakes were killed by the cats and soldiers of St. Pierre. To this day, you'll find monuments on Martinque built to commemorate the cats of St. Pierre.

We are saved not by cats but by a cross. We are healed not by soldiers nor a bronze serpent on a stick but by the grace and love of Jesus Christ. Thanks be to God. Amen.

---

1. Pastor John Eich, "Why God Made You" wwww://forminstry.com/USMIWEVLSGSLCG/sermons/11605.dsp.

Complaint Song

Text: Arley Fadness
music: Ed Johnson

©2003

12
ev - ery where. Grab a drink, not a drop
am no saint. Can't - eat free - dom, once it seemed so fine,
Piano.
15
We could use a so - da pop. Oh,
back to E - gypt where life's di - vine. Oh,
Piano.
17
Coda
bus (out of here)?
Piano.

Manna From Heaven

Object: cans of food

Hi there, good evening, Shalom — Holy Moses here — hello all — I'm back for another time with you. And it's my pleasure to invite children, dads, moms, teens, and a few grandparents to come sit around me.

(traveling music)

Thanks for joining me. Well, we traveled in the wilderness of Sin. Sin is an odd name, but that's what they called it — the Wilderness of Zin. On the fifteenth day of the second month since we left Egypt, the Israelites were hungry. We had no food. The Israelites grumbled. They complained. Came to me, their illustrious leader and cried, "Mr. Holy Moses, we wish we could go back to Egypt where at least we had a Wendy's and a McDonald's."

Well, I spoke to the Lord and the Lord provided a real surprise out there in the wilderness! Would you believe — the Lord rained down manna from heaven. It was a little bread-like wafer and everybody had food! It was like a miracle! Wow! We had never seen anything like it before or since. What a God — a God who provides for our every need!

And you know what? God still provides bread for hungry people today. The Lord does it through you and you and you *(points to the people)*. And here's one way God provides — by giving food to our local food pantry (details may be added). *(shows and hands out a few cans of food)*

Now what will you do with this food? Answer: Give it to _______________ (local description).

God bless you. Amen.

(traveling music)

The Ten Commandments

(Ten Friends Of The Covenant)

Exodus 19:9-20

Characters

Voice Of God (offstage)
Moses
Carnival Barker
Ten Friends

Props

Bell
Placard (xxx@#$$XXX)
Large numerals worn by Friends
"Mount Sinai" sign

Setting

Mount Sinai area

(music)

Scene 1

Moses: Good evening, friends. I am Moses, from the house of Levi. I am pleased to be back with you in this "Holy Moses" Lenten pageant. Come with me. Observe a marvelous incident in the wilderness. We had escaped from Egypt by the mighty hand of God. We wandered in the wilderness *(looks shocked)* would you believe for forty long, hot years? In that time of wandering, God was preparing us for what was to come. And part of what was to come is now. We are at Mount Sinai. It is time to renew the covenant. The Lord speaks to us:

Voice Of God: I am going to come to you, Moses, in a dense cloud, in order that the people may hear when I speak with you and so trust you ever after (Exodus 19:9).

Moses: *(answers)* Trust me ever after? Okay — but that's pretty awesome. *(to the audience)* Well, I told the Lord's message to the people of Israel and then the Lord spoke to me again:

Voice Of God: Go to the people and consecrate them today and tomorrow. Have them wash their clothes and prepare for the third day, because on the third day, I, the Lord will come down upon Mount Sinai in the sight of all the people (cf Exodus 19:10-11).

Moses: Oh my! When I heard that I said, "Offta me, offta my!"

Voice Of God: *(interrupts)* You shall set limits for the people all around, saying, "Be careful not to go up the mountain or to touch the edge of it ... when the trumpet sounds a long blast, they may go up on the mountain" (Exodus 19:12-13).

Moses: So when the Lord finished speaking to me I went down from the mountain to the people. I consecrated the people and they washed their clothes. And I said to the people, "Prepare for the third day...."

On the morning of the third day, there was thunder and lightning, as well as a thick cloud on the mountain, and a blast of a trumpet so loud that all the people who were in the camp trembled. And I was scared too, out of my lovin' mind, but I went up Mount Sinai. And the Lord, almighty and holy, spoke these Ten Commandments:

(Bell toll or chime between each commandment — one bell toll for commandment one, two tolls for two, and so on.)

Friend 1: I am Commandment Number One! Uno! I am the Lord your God, who brought you out of the land of Egypt, out of the house of slavery; you shall have no other gods before me. You shall not make for yourself an idol, whether in the form of anything that is in heaven above, or that is on the earth beneath, or that is in the water under the earth. You shall not bow down to them or worship them; for I the Lord your God am a jealous God, punishing children for the iniquity of parents, to the third and fourth generation of those who reject me, but showing steadfast love to the thousandth generation of those who love me and keep my commandments (cf Exodus 20:2-6).

Barker: *(runs out from the side stage)* And what meaneth that? Pray tell? *(exaggerates comic actions)*

Friend 1: Why hello, Barker, *this* is what it meaneth: *(dramatically)* We are to fear, love, and trust God *above everything* else! And the promise hidden in that command is that God promises to be our God forever.

(Bell tolls or chimes two times.)

Friend 2: I am Commandment Number Two! Dos! You shall not make wrongful use of the name of the Lord your God, for the Lord will not acquit anyone who misuses his name. *(shows placard = xxx@#$$XXX)*

Barker: *(does acrobatics)* And what command from de Lord meaneth that? *(tapes mouth shut)*

Friend 2: *(speaks in a high falsetto voice)* We are to fear and love God so that we do not use his name superstitiously, or use it to curse, swear, lie, or deceive, but call upon him *(Barker pulls off tape on mouth and recites with Friend 2)* in prayer, praise, and thanksgiving!

(Bell tolls or chimes three times.)

Friend 3: I am Commandment Number Tres — that's three for you folks who are limited to English. See — three, three. *(holds up symbols representing three, points to three people, three fingers,* *three hymnals, and the like)* Remember the sabbath day, and keep it holy. Six days you shall labor and do all your work. But the seventh day is a sabbath to the Lord your God ... for in six days the Lord made heaven and earth, the sea, and all that is in them, but rested the seventh day ... (cf Exodus 20:8-11).

Barker: *(mockingly)* And what does the good Doctor Martin Luttter *(use accent)* say about that?

Friend 3: Listen to this, Barker: We are to fear and love God so that we do not neglect his Word and the preaching of it, but regard it as holy, holy, holy, and gladly — that's happily — hear and learn it. In other words "keep in touch" so we can hear the hidden promise of the gospel.

Moses: So the Lord gave the first table of the law, the first three commandments teaching love to God — love to God's person, love to God's name, love to God's holy day. Then came the second table of the Law — love to neighbor. Try these on for size:

(Bell tolls or chimes four times.)

Friend 4: Ta dah! I am Commandment Number Four. Listen up, all you children, and children's children. Honor your father and your mother, so that your days may be long in the land that the Lord your God is giving you (Exodus 20:12). *(looks at Barker)* And that means you, too!

Barker: Huh? Me, too? Okay. *(automatically recites Luther's meaning in a high-toned British accent)* We are to fear and love God so that we do not despise or anger our parents and others in authority, but respect, obey, love, and serve them.

Friend 4: Right on, Barker, right on!

(Bell tolls or chimes five times.)

Friend 5: *(chants)* And I am Commandment Number Five.
I want all to stay alive.
You shall not kill
By a stab or poisonous pill
Nor choke, nor shoot, nor hit
or force anyone into the pit.
(speaks) And that means:

Barker: *(mischievously; also chants)* We are to fear and love God so that, so that, so that ...

Friend 5: Yes, Mr. Barker, go on.

Barker: ... so that we do not hurt our neighbor in any way, but help him in all his physical needs. *(bows)*

Friend 5: Very fine, Barker, very fine.

(Bell tolls or chimes six times.)

Friend 6: *(sings like opera)* And as Commandment Number Six says, chiseled in stone, "You shall not commit adultery."

(Bell tolls or chimes seven times.)

Friend 7: And Commandment Number Seven, "You shall not steal." Does anybody know what these mean? *(looks around and ignores the Barker who jumps up with glee and recites the two meanings)*

Barker: *(high-pitched voice)* We are to fear and love God so that in matters of sex, our words and conduct are pure and honorable, and husband and wife love *(pronounced like Oprah Winfrey does)* and respect each other. *(in a low, bass voice)* We are to fear and love God so that we do not take our neighbor's money or property, or get them in any dishonest way, but help him to improve and protect his property and means of making a living.

Friends 6: That is most certainly true. Good job, Barker. You're pretty smart despite what everybody is saying about you. Ha.

(Bell tolls or chimes eight times.)

Friend 8: I am Commandment Number Eight. You shall not bear false witness against your neighbor (Exodus 20:16) and ... *(quickly recites Luther's meaning before the Barker who is all ready to do it)*

Barker: Uuhhhh ...

Friend 8: We are to fear and love God so that we do not betray, slander, or lie about our neighbor, but defend him, speak well of him, and explain his actions in the kindest way.

(Barker pouts, then changes his/her attitude and gives Friend 8 a hug.)

(Bell tolls or chimes nine, then ten times.)

Friends 9 and 10: *(said together)* We are Commandments Nine and Ten. We are the Covet couple.

Barker: Covet couple?

Friends 9 and 10: Yep, the Covet couple. Don't do it. Don't covet your neighbor's things, inanimate or living but ...

Barker: *(interrupts)* We are to fear, fear, fear and love the Lord God so we do not even desire to get our neighbor's possession or try to coax or tempt away our neighbor's wife or workers but encourage them to remain loyal.

Friends 9 and 10: *You've* got it! Now have *we* got it?

Moses: I hope so. Now, in conclusion, what did God on Mount Sinai say of all these commandments? Listen to this: God threatens to punish all disobedience but in Christ, God sets our futures on a new footing — the promise hidden in the commands. When all the people witnessed the thunder and lightning, the sound of the trumpet, and the mountain smoking, they were afraid and trembled and stood at a distance (Exodus 20:18). I said, "Do not be afraid; for God has come only to test you and to put the fear of him upon you so that you do not sin" (cf Exodus 20:20).

(All bow.)

(music)

Midweek Lent 5 Sermon

Ten Friends Driving Us To The Promise

There is therefore no condemnation for those who are in Christ Jesus. — Romans 8:1

One day last spring, something memorable happened at Carlton University in Ottawa, Ontario, Canada. Thirty-one students in the same class turned in identical research papers. It was determined that the students had all accessed the same internet website.

If only one student had done it, the ruse might not have caught the professor's attention. But here's what else opened the instructor's eyes; the research paper topic was "ethics."

This unethical ethics "research" caper suggests an opportunity. If young people are lacking in moral fiber, where will they get it?[1]

Is there a need for rediscovery of moral footings and a renewed understanding of right and wrong?

When the pope visited Denver for a youth gathering, thousands came. Two young adults sharing a tent in the campsite area said to a reporter that this was the highlight of their spiritual life.

When the reporter asked if they thought the pope would approve of their co-habiting together without the benefit of marriage they replied, "Oh, probably not, but that's his opinion."

Does the pope function and sail on a sea of opinion or is there a higher set of moral guidelines and rules?

Clearly we are sailing on a sea of relativism.

A pastor's daughter recently said, "Well, Dad, what's right for you is right for you but what's right for me is right for me."

Someone says that the best way to show that a stick is crooked is not to spend time arguing about the crookedness but just to put a straight stick alongside it.

You go to a basketball game and soon discover there are no rules. Some dribble, some do not. Fouls are not considered. It's a free for all, its chaos and not a game.

When Moses received the Ten Commandments on Mount Sinai, he received ten friends for Israel's life and journey together. The ten friends taught love of God and love of neighbor.

The first role of these ten friends was to bring order out of chaos. They would assist the people to hear the Word of God and act accordingly.

These ten friends are never out of date. Some of the other levitical, holiness code laws have only contextual application. However, the ten friends Moses received amidst the thunder and lightning on Sinai have universal relevance.

Jim Nestingen writes, "Though the language of the Commandments is seriously dated ... it's reality is as current as morning coffee."[2]

The second role of the Ten Commandments is to require our keeping them. Soon we discover that when our relationship to God is dependant upon human action these friends begin to accuse us.

Professsor Jim Limburg once gave a chapel talk at Augustana College.

His topic was "Moses Makes Me Nervous." He began by reminding the worshipers that Michelangelo's reproduced Moses statue on the Augustana Campus was looking right into Limburg's office window.

Moses makes me nervous, when I am expected to keep the Ten Commandments and my life is judged according to them.

The commandments are demands and when the demands are not met perfectly they clearly show us our sin. They humble us. Break us down. They point out our guilt.

The difference between the Law and the gospel is this: Ask *who* is responsible to fulfill them. The Law (Ten Commandments) says you are. The gospel says *Christ*.

Luther once wrote: "The law says, 'do this,' and it is never done. Grace says, 'believe this,' and everything is already done."[3]

We have come full circle. Unable to believe the promise of the First Commandment, we find ourselves driven out into the world where the Ten Commandments, for all of their reasonableness, turn into indictments. And so we are driven right back to the Promise again, there to obtain the courage and strength — the fear, love, and trust — to live as God's Children."[4]

The third role of the Ten Commandments is to drive us to a Savior. Since obeying the commandments cannot save us, we need a Savior. They drive us to the promise.

They drive us to the gospel in which Christ does it all. Christ has the last word. For the time being, we have to deal with commandments. But there comes a time when the commandments have to end. For as good, life-giving, true and right as they are, finally the commandments double back on themselves, filling us with accusations and denunciations until we cry out in desperation.

Christ is the end of the law. He is the one who can finally say: "Your sin is forgiven. The commandments have finished their work with you."

Every time we quote, memorize, and refer to the Ten Commandments, we thank God for ten honest friends but who are ultimately exchanged for the one friend who is friend of all — Christ our Lord and Savior. Amen.

---

1. "How about giving integrity?" editorial by Michael Scherer, *Metro Lutheran*, 12/3/02 (Minneapolis, Minnesota: Metro Lutheran).

2. James Nestingen, *The Hidden Promise, A Study of the Ten Commandments* (Minneapolis, Minnesota: Augsburg Fortress, 1994).

3. Martin Luther, *Luther's Works*, vol. 31, tr. Harold J. Grimm (Philadelphia: Fortress Press, 1960), p. 56.

4. *Ibid.*

Quails For Supper

Object: blankets made by the church workers

Good evening. Shalom. That's my Hebrew greeting. Peace. I'm Moses, back with you again for this Manna Minute. Glad to be with you. *(a little chatter about Lenten worship, weather, or local happenings)* Now I want to invite you to come forward again like last week.

(traveling music)

To continue the story, we were in the wilderness and the Israelites started to complain again. Complain, complain, complain. Do you ever complain at your house?

These Hebrews were experts at complaining. Here is their complaint: "Manna, Manna, Manna, ugh. We want some meat to eat not just bread." The manna they were eating was like coriander seed, white, and it tasted like wafers made with honey. I liked it.

Nonetheless, I spoke to the Lord, and our gracious Lord, who always provides when we get in a pickle, answered with a promise: "At sunset, a flock of quails will migrate to your camp. Catch them and you'll have plenty of meat. Six days you shall gather the manna and quail, but there will be none available on the sabbath. So the day before gather enough for two days."

Again, boys and girls, ladies and gentlemen, I, Moses, am here to tell you God provided again. And I have a question: How can God use us to provide bread and meat for the poor and hungry and naked and suffering in developing countries around the world?

Here's one way: *(display blankets made for those in need)*

Wow! Thank you for you loving generosity. Please be seated.

(traveling music)

Midweek Lent 6 Drama

News From The *Desert Times*

(The Golden Calf Incident)

Exodus 32; Deuteronomy 9

Characters

Editor of the *Desert Times*
Moses
Reporter
Editor
Staff Writer 1
Staff Writer 2
Paperboy (Papergirl)

Props

Tape recorder
Notebook and pencil
Rock
Optional: an actual paper prepared and delivered to the audience by the paperboy or papergirl

Setting

Wilderness of Zin

(music)

Scene 1

(Moses is walking along, when a reporter approaches him.)

Reporter: Excuse me, sir — sir! Are you the legendary Moses, the Levite, from the family of Kohath, the house of Amram?

Moses: Why, yes, I am.

Reporter: Well, well, so you are the one they call Holy Moses?

Moses: Hmm, I don't know if "holy" is the right description. "Holy" is reserved for our God Yahweh — the God of Abraham, Isaac, and Jacob....

Reporter: Uh, okay, I ...

Moses: *(interrupts) If* I am holy it is because I have been called, dedicated, consecrated, and set apart for a very special mission ...

Reporter: Whatever, Mr. Moses ... *(sweetly)* I'm Bonnie Chunga. I would like to interview you for the *Desert Times*. I'm going to write a feature article on the golden calf incident. You remember the golden calf incident?

Moses: *(explodes)* Remember? How could I forget? It's burned into me like a hot branding iron on the hide of a goat — Oh me, oh my!

Reporter: Quite an emotional thing for you?

Moses: Oh, yes, yes! *(grabs heart, shakes body, rolls eyes)*

Reporter: Good! *(gleefully)* This'll make a great series in the *Desert Times*. Tell me the story. Who, what, when, why, and how? *(tapes Moses and also takes notes)*

Moses: *(sits down on a rock)* Well, Bonnie ... I had gone up Mount Sinai and my return was delayed. The people gathered around my brother, Aaron, he was a priest you know, and they said to him, "Come make gods for us. We don't know what has happened to Moses."

Reporter: Why did they do that?

Moses: *(groans)* Oh, I don't know. I guess they got impatient. I was up there on Sinai for forty days and forty nights. They had no idea when I was coming back, if at all.

Reporter: Go on Moses, sir.

Moses: As it happened, my brother, Aaron, the talker, had everyone donate their gold rings, bracelets, and earrings to the project. They melted all that gold, and fabricated and sculped a golden calf!

Reporter: *(with glee)* A golden calf! Woo woo, this is fascinating.

Moses: I don't think so. *(sadly shakes his head)*

Reporter: *(eagerly)* What happened next?

Moses: The very people I had brought out of the land of Egypt by God's right hand, rose up early the next morning, burned offerings and sacrifices, and then had a party. They gorged themselves and drank too much. They danced the Hebrew honey hop until the wee hours of the morning, making absolute fools of themselves, canceling anything I ever taught them or believed in — ooohhh *(moans)* I was demolished and ...

Reporter: Go on ...

Moses: *(angrily stands up and paces back and forth)* And the Lord, our gracious, kind, and loving Lord, who was giving me the Ten Commandments, cried out, "Moses, quickly go down at once!"

Reporter: And —

Moses: "I am burning hot with anger," the Lord said. "I am so mad at my people whom I brought out of the land of Egypt, that I just might give up on them altogether."

Reporter: *(gleefully)* And then what happened, Mr. Moses?

Moses: I did a two-step down the mountain carrying the two tablets of stone. Remember the First Commandment — You shall have no other gods? I planted that one right in the middle of the dance floor.

Reporter: Wow!

Moses: And I chewed out my brother, Aaron. His ears burned — I made him feel so guilty that he turned red with embarrassment. He was so red, I thought he'd turned into a beet. Then I spent another forty days and forty nights praying to God on behalf of Aaron and the people — and God's hot anger cooled down, thank goodness!

Reporter: And, and the gold calf?

Moses: I threw that imposter in the fire. Burned the gold and all; and that was it!

Reporter: Then what happened?

Moses: I called for a loyalty oath. "Who is on the Lord's side?" I shouted.

Reporter: And ...

Moses: Most of the people stepped up for God, but a lot didn't and they unfortunately were killed. And that's the golden calf incident story.

Reporter: What a story! Thank you, thank you, Mr. Holy Moses. *(gives Moses a hug)* You'll read all about the golden calf incident this Sunday in the *Desert Times. (waves good-bye and runs off stage)*

Scene 2

(In Editor's office, with Editor talking to Staff Writers)

Editor: *(paces)* I need stories! Articles, news items, gossip, anything, the deadline is in four hours! *(looks at watch)*

Staff Writer 1: I have a story.

Editor: Good. Let's hear it!

Staff Writer 1: Fire Station 303 was called out to the Boxer residence at 9:04 last night and rescued the family cat, Tabby, from the neighbor's apple tree and ...

Editor: What kind of junk is that? Don't waste my time with drivel! Get something hot, readable, juicy! That'll never sell papers!

Staff Writer 2: Mr. Editor, I have something.

Editor: *(impatiently)* Spit it out. Let's have it. Times a wastin'.

Staff Writer 2: The Andersons called on the Browns last week and they enjoyed a garden party ... sipping an exotic new tea ...

Editor: Oh, groan. C'mon, staff let's get some blood and guts ...

Reporter: *(comes running in)* I've got it. I've got it!

Staff Writer 1: Really?

Editor: Got what?

Reporter: I've got a doozy! The holy man, Moses, and his talking brother, Aaron — a real scandal!

Editor and Staff Writers: Scandal? Really?

Editor: *(eagerly)* GRRReeaaat! Is it factual? Front page stuff?

Reporter: Yes, sir!

Editor: We don't want to get sued. We're not the *National Inquirer* you know. *(laughs nervously)*

(all staff laughs nervously, mocking their boss)

Reporter: Well, Moses, the man of God, went up on Mount Sinai out there in the wilderness and no sooner had he gotten there when ...

(musical interlude continues while the Reporter tells the story)

Reporter: And that is the incident of the golden calf in the Wilderness of Zin.

Editor: Wow! Great, Bonnie! Let the presses roll! What else has anybody got?

Staff Writer 1: I have an ad:

Wanted: New Tablets of Stone. Originals broken. Price no object. Please deliver to the following Mount Sinai address. Wear dark glasses when delivering due to extreme shining.

Editor: *(excitedly)* Great! Put it in the Want Ad section. Anything else?

Staff Writer 2: Yes, sir, here's what I have for the religious section:

Day of Atonement Set. Yom Kippur to be celebrated by all repentant Israelites. Come with ashes and sackcloth. The public — whoever can repent — is invited!

Editor: Anything else?

Staff Writer 1: Yes, a second news article in the religious section:

Sabbatical expanded to the Jubilee Year. There will be seven Sabbaticals making 49 years. Every fiftieth year will be declared a year of rest for the land, for slaves, and for all. All debts will be forgiven and a new social order will begin in which all are equal.

Editor: The slaves will love it. The bankers will scream. But it's the public who'll read this story. Great!

Staff Writer 2: I wrote the obituary, although the subject is still alive.

Editor: Read it.

Staff Writer 2: *(reads Deuteronomy 34:1-10)* Then Moses went up from the plains of Moab to Mount Nebo to the top of Pisgah, which is opposite Jericho, and the Lord showed him the whole land: Gilead as far as Dan, all Naphtali, the land of Ephraim and Manasseh, all the land of Judah as far as the Western Sea, the Negeb and the Plain — that is, the valley of Jericho, the city of Palm trees — as far as Zoar. The Lord said to [Moses], "This is the land of which I swore to Abraham, to Isaac, and to Jacob, saying, I will give it to your descendents; I have let you see it with your eyes, but you shall not cross over there."

Then Moses the servant of the Lord, died there in the land of Moab, at the Lord's command. He was buried in a valley in the land of Moah opposite Beth-peor, but no one knows his burial place to this day. Moses was one hundred twenty years old when he died; his sight was unimpaired and his vigor had not abated.

The Israelites wept for Moses in the plains of Moab thirty days; ... never since has there arisen such a prophet in Israel like Moses whom the Lord knew face to face.

Editor: That's great! Staff, I think we have it! The best edition yet! Let the presses roll!

(Editor dances a jig and soon the entire staff is doing the bunny hop)

Paperboy or Papergirl: *(out in the audience)* Extra, extra. Read all about it! Right here in the *Desert Times*. Fifty cents. Read all about the golden calf incident. Read all about the final days of Holy Moses. Extra, extra!

(Sing the "Holy Moses" theme song.)

Midweek Lent 6 Sermon

Promises Broken/Promises Mended

Exodus 32; Deuteronomy 9:17, 18, 26; Hebrews 8:6

Our son flipped an object across the room one day, and it struck a pedestaled Fostoria cake dish sitting on our old hutch. The cake dish, a wedding gift from a favorite aunt and uncle, shattered into a thousand pieces. Unmendable, we shoveled it into the trash.

Marriages, too, are often broken like this wedding cake dish. The promises made and sealed with a kiss fall to the floor, signaling the death of a promised relationship.

The story of the golden calf is the story of broken promises and broken covenants. God's covenants with Israel began with Abraham and Sarah. "I will make of you a great nation and I will bless and make your name great, so that you will be a blessing."

There were other covenants with Noah, and with David. Now this covenant with Moses which begins with, "If you obey my voice and keep my covenant you shall be a special treasure...." God kept God's promises, but Israel ... well, not so.

The incident started when Moses went up Mount Sinai to receive the Sinaitic Covenant — the Ten Commandments. Moses' return was delayed. The people of Israel grew impatient. Forty days and forty nights — no Moses. Had he died up there? Had he been attacked by a wild animal? Had he given up on the Israelites and left for good?

Moses was their access to God. No Moses, no access to God. They turned to Aaron, "Aaron, Aaron, come make gods for us." And Aaron did. Aaron made a golden calf like the Canaanite fertility bull. Aaron took their jewelry, earrings, and bracelets, and melted them down and set before them a god they could touch and feel and see — this beautiful golden calf.

The people were excited. They ate, drank, danced, and reveled in a frenzy around their new god.

When Moses returned at last, he exploded — he knew God was angry and he smashed the two tablets upon which the finger of God had written the Ten Commandments. The tablets broke up into a pile of rocks. The covenant was broken.

What broke the promises of God? The people's impatience, to be sure. Their stubbornness. The biblical image for stubborn is "stiff-necked" and refers to a horse who resists the reins and will not yield to it's rider. Their lack of trust, their lack of obedience, their rebelliousness, but, most of all, their thirst for a religious experience, even if it is a counterfeit.

We, too, have our golden calves — whole herds. Like Israel, the prodigal nation, and the prodigal son, we are empty, longing, and yearning to be filled with purpose and meaning. The spiritual void must be filled with authenticity or we will find something counterfeit to fill it.

Often we misinterpret our deepest longings and seek fulfillment in strange ways. We sculpt golden calves, seeking fulfillment through shopping, eating, adultery, or becoming addicts to work, alcohol, drugs, pornography, all in our quest to be filled and to be satisfied.

Jesus taught that humanity was after something great: "Life — eternal life, that we may know thee."

Saint Augustine said the same thing, "Thou hast made us for thyself, O God, and restless are our souls until they rest in thee."

Look around. The rocks from the broken tablets lay strewn about. Other gods creeping in because we pollute God's holy name, over schedule God's sabbath, ignore our parents and others in authority, show little reverence for life, and seek to satisfy sexual appetites. It is true, we are thieves, we lie, we cheat, and we covet.

James took a deep breath and wrote in 2:10, "For whoever keeps the whole law but fails in one point has become accountable for all of it." A fresh wind blows whenever we hear, "For God so loved the world that he gave his only begotten son...." The new covenant is in Jesus. It is the new and eternal covenant. It is God's promise that God keeps through grace.

The Fostoria cake dish is gone. The two tablets are also gone. Christ is the new covenant.

When Natalie Wood died at age 43, a distraught Robert Wagner was comforted by his doctor who quoted a line from Eugene O'Neill, "Man is broken. He lives by mending. And the grace of God is the glue." Amen.

Saved By An Image On A Pole

Object: crutch, pamphlets from Church World Service or Lutheran World Relief

Hi, all — Holy Moses here! *(enters on a crutch)* Welcome to our last Lenten worship. It's been fun to see you and meet you these past weeks. Now I invite the children, parents, and grandparents to join me here up front for our Manna Minute.

(traveling music)

We had some harrowing experiences out there in the desert. Today you heard about the golden calf incident.

I remember a while back in the wilderness when the snakes came. Those poisonous serpents bit us for all the grumbling we did. The Lord told me to erect a bronze serpent on a pole and I did. The Lord told me to tell the people who had been bitten to look at the bronze serpent and they would not die but would be healed.

We didn't know it at the time but this act prefigured the coming of Christ who would be put up on a cross and whoever looked to him for salvation would be saved.

In your day and time, there is something worse than a snake hidden in the ground in a lot of places in the world. It's the left over mines from war in Cambodia, Vietnam, and lots of other places. Little children or adults can step on a mine and hurt their legs or destroy them. My leg is okay, but this crutch is a visual reminder of what happens again and again.

There are ministries through Church World Service and Lutheran World Relief that are helping to get rid of these terrible weapons.

(traveling music)

www.ingramcontent.com/pod-product-compliance
Lightning Source LLC
LaVergne TN
LVHW020652100826
845148LV00012B/2440